William Berry Lapham

Bar Harbor and Mount Desert Island

William Berry Lapham

Bar Harbor and Mount Desert Island

ISBN/EAN: 9783744733526

Printed in Europe, USA, Canada, Australia, Japan

Cover: Foto ©ninafisch / pixelio.de

More available books at **www.hansebooks.com**

AND

Mount Desert Island.

"*An island full of hills and dells*
All rumpled and uneven."

"*The gray and thunder-smitten pine*
Which marks afar the Desert Isle."

PRESS OF LIBERTY PRINTING COMPANY

107 Liberty Street, New York.

PREFACE.

NOT much of the history of Mount Desert is contained in the following pages. To relate the story of this wonderful Island and its people would require a large volume. Nor is it claimed that much is contained here which has not already appeared in some other form. The purpose of these few pages is to give, in a brief and concise form, a description of some of the more interesting places found here, to describe briefly the physical features of the Island, its bold and rock-bound shores, its coves, harbors and bays, its mysterious caverns, its wonderful mountains, its highland ponds and lakes, its curious geological formation, and, in addition, to give a few of the more salient points in its civil history, and the marvelous growth of Bar Harbor and vicinity as a summer resort. It is hoped that the matter is presented in a form that will be found intelligible, and that the numerous questions which are sure to be asked by those who contemplate visiting Bar Harbor, or those who do visit it for the first time, are here satisfactorily answered.

W. B. L.

AUGUSTA, 1886.

Bar Harbor.

O F all the numerous nooks and corners on the North Atlantic coast which have become famous as seaside resorts, there is none whose growth has been more rapid than that of Bar Harbor. Less than a score of years ago it was unknown to the great world of pleasure seekers. True, it had been visited by a few artists, who had found their way across from Southwest Harbor by way of Somes' Sound, and who, attracted by its marvelous scenery, had remained here for the purpose of transferring some of its unique views to canvas. It was through these views that the scenery along this wild and rock-bound coast, became somewhat familiar to the dwellers in the great cities, and turned the tide of summer travel in this direction. There was a little hamlet here prior to 1867, and Tobias Roberts had a boat landing and kept a little store for the convenience of the few straggling settlers on this side of the island. Since that time the development and growth of the place has been almost phenomenal, and in the brief space of eighteen years, it has become one of the most popular summer resorts on the entire coast, rivalling such old established places as Newport, Nahant and Long Branch.

In 1866, Capt. Charles Deering began running the steamer "City of Richmond" from Portland to Machiasport, touching at Rockland, Castine, Deer Isle and Southwest Harbor. He had previously, and as early as 1854, commanded the steamer "T. F. Secor," which plied between Bangor and Machiasport. The popular demand for a more direct communication to Bar Harbor was responded to by the erection of a convenient wharf, and in 1868 Capt. Deering commenced touching at this point. This wharf was built by Tobias Roberts, assisted by Capt. Deering, and the steamer "Lewiston" was the first boat to make regular trips to Bar Harbor.

The wharf was subsequently purchased by the Eastern Railroad Company, and greatly enlarged; it is the principal wharf there at the

BAR HARBOR, MOUNT DESERT, ME.

present time. Roberts erected a small hotel, the Agamont House, and the first in the place, in 1867. The steamers " Lewiston " and "City of Richmond " are owned and run by the Portland, Bangor, Mount Desert and Machias Steamboat Company, although in 1884, the line, including all other property of the corporation, was purchased by the Maine Central Railroad Company, who now operate it under the old name and as a separate company.

Bar Harbor took its name from the fact that at low water a bar is exposed between this island and Bar Island, sometimes called Rodick's Island. With improved facilities for reaching here the influx of visitors rapidly increased, and hotel accommodations were correspondingly enlarged. The nucleus of the present Rodick House was built in 1867, by Daniel Rodick, formerly of Rodick's Island, where his ancestor settled prior to 1776. In 1870, 1875, and in 1882, this house was enlarged, until its present capacity is six hundred or more guests. The Bay View House was built in 1869, and after being enlarged several times, was changed to the Grand Central. The Atlantic House was built in 1870, burned and re-built larger in 1873; the Newport was built in 1871, the St. Sauveur was re-built after having been burned, in 1872, the Rockaway in 1873, the Marlborough, formerly the Deering, about the same time, the Ocean House in 1874, the Belmont in 1879, and the West End a little later. Then there are the Des Isle, the Malvern, the Lynam Cottages, several other smaller houses and more to be built whenever they shall be needed.

The following table shows approximately the number of the larger hotels, their capacity and the names of proprietors:

Rodick,	-	-	D. Rodick & Sons,	600
West End, -	-	-	O. M. Shaw & Son,	300
Rockaway,	-	-	T. L. Roberts,	100
Newport,	-	-	W. M. Roberts,	100
Marlborough, -		-	Charles Higgins,	100
Atlantic, -	-	-	E. T. Hamor,	100
Ocean,	-	-	Samuel Higgins,	40
Grand Central,	-	-	R. Hamor & Sons,	350
Hotel Des Isle,		-	A. I. Saunders,	75
Lynam Cottages, -		-	J. S. Lynam,	100
Belmont,	-	-	J. C. Manchester,	75
Lookout, -	-	-	S. S. Salisbury,	40
St. Sauveur,	-	-	Alley Brothers,	175
Malvern, -	-	-	De Grasse Fox,	—
Hamilton,	-		G. W. Hamilton,	40
Exchange,	-	-	W. C. Higgins,	40
Birch Tree,	-	-	J. A. Rodick,	50
Wayside,	-	-	Mrs. R. G. Higgins,	35

All these hotels are pleasantly located, and with special reference to sea and harbor views, and besides these hotels there are nearly seventy-five cottages rented to visitors.

The first cottage erected as a summer residence was built on Hardy's Point, by Alpheus Hardy of Boston, in 1867, and this is still standing. Since that time a large number of elegant cottages have been built, broad streets and avenues have been laid out and constructed, elegant residences have been built upon the cliffs and bluffs, and the landscape which twenty years ago was a barren waste, and almost worthless, has been transformed into a large and beautiful village. Land has advanced in price a thousand fold, and choice building lots will command almost any sum asked. The following list comprises the names of the streets, and most of the cottages at Bar Harbor and vicinity, with names of the owners or occupants during the season of 1885, although the list is by no means complete:

ALBERT AVENUE.

A. Higgins' Cottage,	- -	Parke Goodwin,	New York.
A. Higgins' Cottage,	- - -	Charles Payson,	Washington, D. C.

ATLANTIC AVENUE.

Brewer Cottage,	- - -	H. La Barre Jayne,	Philadelphia.
	- - -	Dr. Horace Jayne,	Philadelphia.
John Suminsby Cottage,	- -	Miss Weidenfeld,	New York.
Tripp Cottage,	- - -	Miss E. C. White,	Philadelphia.
Thurber Cottage,	- - -	Dr. S. M. Miller,	Philadelphia.

BIRCH POINT AND THE BAY SHORE.

Ambrose Higgins' Cottage,	- -	Miss Buchanan,	
Birch Point,	- - - -	Alpheus Hardy,	Boston.
Baltimore Cottages,	- - -	Miss Buchanan,	
Derby Cottage,	- - -	Dr. Haskett Derby,	Boston.
Dove Cottage,	- - - -	W. P. Walley,	Andover, Mass.
Dillingham Cottage,	- - -	F. A. Wilson,	Bangor, Me.
Edgemere,	- - - - -	T. B. Musgrave,	New York.
Fernierest,	- - -	Wm. F. Cochran,	Yonkers, N. Y.
Grant Cottage,	- - - -	H. A. Grant,	Tarrytown, N. Y.
Jones Cottage,	- - - -	F. R. Jones,	New York.
Minot Cottage,	- - - -	George R. Minot,	
Weld Cottage,	- - - -	Rev. F. G. Peabody,	Camb'ge, Mass.
Weld Cottage,	- - - -	Mrs. F. M. Field,	Boston, Mass.

COTTAGE STREET.

Andrew Rodick Cottage,	- -	J. M. P. Price,	Camden, N. J.
Andrew Rodick Cottage,	- -	Mrs. William Stroud,	Philadelphia.

Aunt Charlotte's Cottage,	-	Mrs. Henry Armitt Brown,	Phila.
Longstreth Cottage, -	-	Dr. Morris Longstreth,	"
Mrs. Stubb's Cottage,	- -	Dr. John G. Curtis,	New York.
" "	- - -	Mrs. G. R. Davis,	New York.
" "	- -	Mr. Lindsey Bury,	Mandarin, Fla.
" "	- - -	Mr. Robert Neilson,	Philadelphia.
" "	- -	Mrs. James P. Chadwick,	Boston.
Manchester Cottage, -	- -	Thomas Janney,	Baltimore.
Rodick Cottage, No. 1,	- -	John B. Morris,	"
Salisbury Cottage,	- - -	Mrs. H. Winter Davis,	"

CLEFTSTONE ROAD.

Cleftstone,	- - - -	Isaac W. How,	New York.
Mizzentop, -	- - - -	J. Arthur Beebe,	Boston.
Mizzentop,	- - -	Mrs. W. D. Peachy,	Washington.

DES ISLE AVENUE.

Anderson Cottage,	- -	Mrs. Clymer	New York.
Des Isle Cottage,	- -	Col. Royall,	Washington.
S. H. Leland Cottage,	-	Capt. G. M. Wheeler,	Washington.

DUCK BROOK.

Baymeath,	- - -	John De Koven,	Chicago.
Edenfield, -	- - -	Samuel E. Lyon,	New York.
Sonogee, -	- - -	Mrs. D. H. Haight,	"
Sonogee,	- - - -	Mrs. D. K. Granger,	".

EAGLE LAKE ROAD.

Homewood,	- - -	Mrs. John Saunders,	Philadelphia.
Lookout,	- - - -	Mr. Robinson,	Philadelphia.
Stanton Cottage,	- -	Mrs. Stanton,	Washington, D.C.
The Knoll, -	- - -	Mrs. Wilkins,	Philadelphia.

EDEN STREET AND VICINITY.

Bagatelle,	- - -	{ Mr. and Mrs. Edmund Pendleton, Cincinnati, Ohio.
Brigham Bungalow,	- -	Wm. T. Brigham.
Clovercroft,	- - -	Mrs. George Place, New York.
Eddy Cottage,	- - -	James Eddy, Providence, R. I.
Fox Cottage, -	- -	De Grasse Fox, Philadelphia.
Lombard Cottage,	- -	The Misses Lombard, Boston.
Villa Mary, -	- -	Rev. F. H. Johnson, Philadelphia.
Witch Clyffe,	- - -	Mrs. F. C. Manning, Boston.

HIGHBROOK ROAD.

Highbrook, - - - -	Mrs. James Leeds,	Boston.
Mossley Hall, - - - -	W. B. Howard,	Chicago.

HANCOCK STREET.

Barron Cottage, - - -	Mrs. C. Morton Smith,	Philadelphia.
Wyandotte, - - - - -	Mr. J. Biddle Porter,	Philadelphia.
Devilstone, - - - -	Geo. W. Vanderbilt and family,	N.Y.
Devilstone, - - - - -	Wm. H. Vanderbilt,	New York.

HOLLAND AVENUE.

A. Higgins' Cottage, - -	Mr. Ryerson,	Chicago, Ill.
Ansel Leland Cottage. - -	Mrs. R L. Fabian,	New York.
Eri Bunker Cottage, - -	Mrs. H. C. Beach,	New York.
Ells Cottage, - - - -	Dr. Hutchinson,	Philadelphia.

KEBO STREET.

Richardson Cottage. - -	Mrs. John Whitaker, St. Louis, Mo.	
Kebo Cottage, - - -	Mrs. J. W. Minturn,	New York.
" " - - - -	J. Lawrence Aspinwall,	"
" " - - - -	Hamilton L. Hoppin,	"

MOUNT DESERT STREET AND VICINITY.

Cunningham Cottage, - -	Miss L. Delafield,	New York.
Curtis Cottage, - - -	Prof. Geo. Harris, Andover, Mass.	
Ledge Lawn, - - - -	Miss M. C. Shannon, Newton, Mass.	
Muller Cottage, - - -	Mr. Robbins,	New York.
Orlando Ash Cottage, - -	Mr. James P. Scott, Philadelphia.	
Parker Cottage, - - -	Mrs. Edward Gardiner,	Boston.
Primrose " - - -	Mrs. A. J. Pendleton, Philadelphia.	
Shingle " - - -	Rev. William Lawrence,	Boston.
The Craigs, - - - -	Mr. James S. Amory,	Boston.
The Eyrie, - - - -	Dr. Robert Amory, Brookline, Mass.	

MAIN STREET.

Brewer Cottage, - - -	Mrs. Daniel Wetmore,	New York.
H. Higgins' Cottage, - -	Mrs. M. G. Evans,	New York.
Mrs. M. I. Higgins' Cottage, -	Mrs. R. Snowden Andrews, Baltim'e.	

MALDEN HILL.

Toppingwold, - - - -	F. W. Lawrence, Brookline, Mass.	
Thirlstane, - - - -	Mrs. R. B. Scott, Washington, D. C.	

OGDEN POINT AND VICINITY.

Aldersea, - - - - -	Edward Coles,	Philadelphia.
Watersmeet, - - - -	Mrs. G. M. Ogden,	New York.

SCHOOL STREET.

Cristie Cottage, - - - -	Charles Dennison,	New York.

SCHOONER HEAD.

Hale Cottage, - - - -	George S. Hale,	Boston.

THE FIELD.

Carey Cottage, - - - -	Prof. H. N. Martin,	Baltimore.
Geo. Higgins' Cottage, - -	J. P. Norris,	New York.
L. Higgins' " - -	Dr. Wm. Todd Helmuth,	"
L. Higgins' " - -	Lieut. W. P. Edgarton,	"
Ocean " - -	Mrs. Crehore,	Boston.
Stephen Higgins' Cottage, -	Mrs. Van Buren,	New York.
Yellow House, - - - -	Mrs. T. C. A. Linzee,	Boston.

WOODBURY PARK.

Guy's Cliff, - - - -	E. C. Cushman,	Newport, R. I.
Beau Desert, - - - -	W. S. Gurnee,	New York.

It will be noticed that among those who have either owned or occupied cottages here are some of the most distinguished men of the country. The Vanderbilts, the Ogdens, the Musgraves, the Howards, the Amorys, the Sears, and the Harrises are well known in financial circles; Bishop Doane of New York and President Eliot of Harvard College have cottages on this island, and Hon. James G. Blaine has purchased a lot, and will have Stanwood Cottage ready for occupancy early this summer. Some of these cottages cost not less than $100,000 each, and a large sum of money has been put into these temporary dwellings.

Since the opening of the Mount Desert Branch of the Maine Central Railroad, a new impulse has been given to the travel in this direction, and the number of visitors to Bar Harbor has more than quadrupled within the last two years, and is yearly increasing.

Bar Harbor as a summer resort, owes its popularity to its pure bracing air, its romantic and extended driveways, its enchanting ocean views and its grand mountain scenery. The cool currents from the Arctic seas reach these shores, modifying the temperature so that the heat rarely, if ever, becomes oppressive. Eagle Lake, embosomed among the mountains, and fed by crystal streams and bubbling springs, supplies the village with the purest of water; this lake is 275 feet above the sea-level, and a jet of water from any of the numerous hydrants can be thrown to a perpendicular height of more than seventy-five feet. This affords ample protection against fire, a matter of no small consideration where the large hotels and most of the other buildings are constructed of wood.

EAGLE LAKE

Main Street is largely devoted to stores and shops, and groceries, dry and fancy goods, boots and shoes, and clothing can be purchased here at as low a price as they can in Bangor or Portland. Electric light has been introduced and all other modern improvements have been made. A first-class weekly paper, the Mount Desert *Herald*, is published by Joseph Wood.

HOW TO REACH BAR HARBOR.

No longer as in days gone by, is the visitor obliged to cross the Island from Southwest Harbor by the circuitous route, through Somesville nor, as later, to depend upon a single line of steamers, making the trip two or three times a week, to reach Bar Harbor, for since 1884, there is an all-rail route to within eight miles of Bar Harbor wharf, and safe ferry boats always in waiting to convey passengers across the intervening space, known as Frenchman's Bay. The Mount Desert Branch of the Maine Central Railroad is forty-two miles in length. Crossing the Penobscot river at Bangor, it passes through the towns of Brewer, Holden, Dedham, Ellsworth and Hancock to the terminus at Hancock Point. The most remarkable feature along this route is an immense train of boulders which the road crosses diagonally, entering it in the town of Holden and leaving it near Reed's Upper Pond in Dedham. From the car windows these piles of boulders can be seen, varying in weight from a few pounds to hundreds of tons, and crowded together so as to obstruct all vegetation, and resembling a huge dilapidated stone wall. At some points immense blocks of granite are so evenly poised as almost to threaten the safety of the railroad track. None of these rocks are in place, but their appearance here is unquestionably the result of glacial action. They constitute an ancient moraine whose general direction is from Northeast to Southwest. It begins from the point where the railway crosses it, toward Moosehead Lake, and terminates in a gravelly deposit in the town of Orland. Ellsworth Falls is a thriving village where power is obtained from Union river and a large lumber business is carried on, and Ellsworth, the next station, is a beautiful little city situated at the head of navigation on the same river. Hancock Village with its neat white cottages is soon passed, and the next and last station is Mount Desert Ferry, situated on the easterly side of Frenchman's Bay. During the past season Bangor parties have erected an elegant hotel at this point which will doubtless become a popular resort. It is built upon a bluff near the railway station, and rightly named "the Bluffs," has delightful surroundings, and a fine view of the bay. Here the passengers leave the cars, embark on board the commodious ferry boat which, with steam up, is waiting, and after half an hour's sail, inhaling the cooling and refreshing breeze from the open sea, the bay is crossed and Bar Harbor is reached. Passengers can leave Boston in elegant palace cars at nine o'clock in the morning and before eight the same evening they can be at their hotel or cottage at Bar Harbor. Or they can leave Boston at seven o'clock in the evening by sleeping cars, arrive in Bangor at five-thirty the following morning and at Bar Harbor at eight-thirty. The day train during the excursion season is a fast

MOUNT DESERT FROM "THE BLUFFS." MOUNT DESERT FERRY.

express, and makes the distance between Boston and Bangor, including all stops in less than eight hours.

Persons preferring the water route can take the steamers "City of Richmond" or "Lewiston" at Portland, which make the round trip between Portland and Machiasport twice a week, stopping at Bar Harbor and all places of importance along the coast. This route has the advantage of enabling one to view the grand scenery which is unfolded from every side from the time Rockland is left until Bar Harbor is reached.

PLACES HISTORIC AND PICTURESQUE.

Many of the summer residents at Bar Harbor content themselves with remaining in the vicinity of the village, and spend the whole season, and season after season without visiting other points of interest, while others do not like to settle down to the quiet of cottage life until all the mysteries of the Island have been explored. To such as enjoy visiting the outlying nooks and corners, there is every facility for doing so. The roads are magnificent, the gravelly soil of the Island being the best of material for making them. Large sums of money have been expended in road-making, and they are everywhere excellent. Then there are always teams in waiting, buck-boards, cutaways and carryalls, with one or two horses as may be desired, and the cupidity of the owner is held in check by municipal authority, the price per diem to each point to be visited being established and a printed list furnished to those desiring it.

GREEN MOUNTAIN.

The first point of interest is Green Mountain, the highest point on the Island. Some ambitious persons make the ascent on foot, and that can best be done by way of the ruins of the old mill near the foot of Mount Kebo, and then by way of the ravine that separates Green from Dry Mountain. But by far the largest number prefer to go by the regular conveyance furnished by the Green Mountain Railway which is by carriage to Eagle Lake, thence by steamer up the lake to the base, then by railway to the summit. This gives variety to the trip which is a most enjoyable one. A clear bright morning should be selected for this excursion, when objects can be seen at a great distance. The railway itself is a marvel of engineering skill, the entire length of the road being six thousand three hundred feet, and the grade averaging one foot to every four feet passed over. There is a good hotel at the summit which will accommodate about thirty guests.

The view from Green Mountain, on a clear morning, is one never to be forgotten. The coast line with its many sinuosities, the numerous smaller islands scattered here and there, Mount Desert spread out like a map and the inland landscape with its diversity of views, all go to make

up a succession of the grandest pictures imaginable. One familiar with the history and legends of this wonderful Island, as he stands upon this rocky eminence and glances over its sea cradled islands, its sun-burnished creeks, its mountain lakes and its alp-like ravines, may easily imagine that a savage is about to emerge from some glen, or to see lying at anchor, the rude shallop of two hundred years ago; or still stranger to behold some wanderer from across the sea in the habiliment of his time, with steeple hat, peaked beard, slashed doublet and sword by his side, climbing the sea-wall to seek his rude cabin on the shore.

SCHOONER HEAD.

There is a legend that in the war of 1812 a British frigate ran towards the shore at this point and opened fire upon what was supposed to be a schooner, but which was simply a white formation on a dark ground. Schooner Head is four miles from Bar Harbor, the road being the one nearest the easterly side of the Island. It is a spur of Newport Mountain, and appears as a bare almost perpendicular headland, about a hundred feet high, on the eastern face of which is still to be seen the large white figure which, out at sea, looks like a schooner with her three lower sails set. In the top of the cliff, at the left, is a deep cleft, with a passage at its bottom worn through the rock to low water mark, through which, during a severe southerly storm, the surf passes upward with a rush and roar, and is driven with great force above the tops of the trees. This is known as "Spouting Horn." Across a little cove, toward the south, is Anemone Cave, a wonderful grotto where each succeeding tide deposits strange creatures from the sea, including the polyp, known as the sea anemone, which remain stranded among rockweed and mosses, when the water recedes.

GREAT HEAD.

A little farther westward is Great Head which shelters the only beach on the Island and a very small one at that. Great Head is a prominent object when passing from Bar Harbor to Southwest Harbor by water. "No description can do justice to its savage grandeur. It is not to its height alone that it owes its impressiveness, but to the peculiar massiveness of the rocks, the overhanging of the whole cliff, and the never-ceasing beat and roar of the waves below."

OTTER CLIFFS.

The drive from Bar Harbor to the Otter Cliffs is five miles, and the road, nearly parallel with that to Schooner Head, is through the deep narrow gorge between Newport and Dry Mountains. There is a little hamlet and a red granite quarry on the left side of Otter Creek, and passing these, Mr. Robert Young has closed up the way by a gate, and contends for his right of eminent domain by demanding ten cents for the right to cross his premises to the Cliffs. Otter Creek Point is the southeastern extremity of the Island, and when seen from the eastward, appears as a thickly wooded neck of land arising to a height of about two hundred feet, with a precipitous face over one hundred feet high on its eastern side, which are the "Cliffs." To the north of this point

about a mile is a wooded eminence five hundred feet high called Otter Peak. This is a delightful drive and can be accomplished in a short half day.

HULL'S COVE.

This is a large indentation on the eastern face of the Island about three-eighths of a mile wide and situated some four miles north of Bar Harbor. There is an old settlement here, and a small unfinished vessel was upon the stocks at the time of our visit. An anchorage for small vessels is afforded here,

EN ROUTE TO THE CLIFFS.

but the place is not of much account. The early settlers were mostly engaged in fishing, but little of this business is carried on here now. A large mansion house here, erected many years ago by the Hamor family, is constructed of brick burned in the vicinity. It was at Hull's Cove that the French grantees of the Island lived, and here Madame Theresa Gregoire, grand-daughter of Cadillac the grantee, died in 1810. Her husband had previously deceased and after her death, the family returned to France.

THE OVENS.

From Hull's Cove to Sand's Point, which is the northeastern extremity of Mount Desert Island, the shore curves gradually around to the northward and thence to the northwestward, forming a large headland or cape, about a mile and three-quarters in diameter, the height varying from eighty to two hundred and twenty feet. Near Sand's

THE OVENS.

Point and just to the south of it are bold perpendicular rocky cliffs, with numerous caves in the eastern face called the "Ovens." When the tide is out a pebbly beach is found at the foot of the cliffs nearly a hundred feet wide, along which are the entrances to these shallow caves, which by the action of the water appear in every variety of form. At one point, a column is left standing which seems to aid in supporting the huge overhanging cliff. The pebbles on the beach are formed by the action of the waves, from the fragments of rock torn from the face of the cliff, and are found in curious forms and shapes. These Ovens are visited by large numbers, but the tide-table should be carefully consulted before visiting them, as in high water, the Ovens are full and inaccessible.

SALISBURY COVE.

From Sand's Point almost due west, and some two or three miles distant, is Salisbury Cove, so named from an early settler here. This is the harbor of the town of Eden, and has an anchorage for vessels of large draught. There is a town-house here, and the citizens of Bar Harbor and other parts of the town of Eden are obliged to come here to exercise the right of suffrage. It is a pleasant place and one of the best farming localities on the Island. Upon the head-stones at the little cemetery near the town-house are found the names of John Ebenezer and Nathan Salisbury, Abner Young, Capt. Isaac Hopkins, Nicholas Richardson and Johnathan Doane; also Cousins, Harden, Liscomb and others, showing who were the pioneer settlers of this region. The return is most of the way by a road recently built.

TWENTY-TWO MILE DRIVE.

What is known as the twenty-two mile drive will occupy a good half day when saving of time is an object, but to do full justice to all the points of interest, it should occupy an entire day. Leaving Bar Harbor and travelling westward, Eagle point is the first point of interest, but this has already been spoken of in connection with the Green Mountain Railway. Leaving this at the left, the road soon bears to the right, toward the head of Somes' Sound. Along this road a fine view of Eagle Lake, Green Mountain, and the railway up its rugged side, can he had. By going a little out of the way around the head of Somes' Sound, the beautiful village of Somesville is reached. Here was where Abraham Somes, Jr., settled in 1762 and where his posterity for four generations have lived or still live. An account of this settlement will appear further along. Returning around the head of the Sound, the road leads down by its easterly side between Brown's and Hadlock's Mountains, by Hadlock's Pond, through beautiful stretches of woodland to

NORTHEAST HARBOR,

The entrance to which is five-eighths of a mile from Gilpatrick's Point. There are good hotels here—the Kimball House, Revere Hotel, Harbor Cottage and Robert's House—and near is Bishop Doane's cottage and chapel and President Eliot's cottage. The shores of the harbor are mostly and thickly wooded, and at the eastern point of entrance is a white sand beach, where it joins the higher lands. The cottages referred to are situated on high and commanding ground overlooking the harbor and having a distant view of the open sea. It has been supposed by some that Northeast Harbor was the place where the early Jesuit mission was established, but the description of the place given in Biard's Journal in no respect corresponds with it.

SEAL HARBOR.

Leaving Northeast Harbor we are on the home stretch and the next point of interest is Seal Harbor, the road leading first southerly and then easterly and passing between Bracy's Cove and the foot of Long Pond, while seaward is seen Bear Island with its light-house and Sutton's Island. Near Long Pond Post Office, a road branches to the left, leading by the "Triads" to Jordan's Pond which is situated at the western base of Pemetic Mountain. Seal Cove is situated a mile and a half to the westward of Otter Creek, is ledgy and has only from two to three fathoms of water. There are low islets at its mouth and a few houses on its shores, the owners of which are engaged more or less in fishing. Summer residents have already begun to gather at the Sea Petite and other Hotels, and like all other points around the Island, it has attractions peculiar to itself. From here the road leads by the Clefts to the head of Otter Creek, and across the line between Mount Desert and Eden, passing the Peak of Otter and intersecting with the Otter Creek road just north of the Beehive.

"AROUND THE ISLAND" TRIP.

If one is pressed for time, the circuit of the entire Island can be made in two days, and all the points of interest visited. Leaving Bar Harbor in the morning, visiting Hull's Cove, Sand's Point including the Ovens, Salisbury Cove, Emory's Cove, Hadley's Point and Thomas' Bay, Mount Desert Narrows is reached. The narrows is spanned by a bridge seven hundred feet in length, connecting the Island with Trenton on the mainland. This bridge has a draw for the passage of vessels. Frenchman's Bay terminates at the narrows and Western Bay begins.

PRETTY MARSH HARBOR.

Leaving Clark's Cove, Indian Point, High-head (208 feet) Squid and Mill Coves on the right, the road leads by Pretty Marsh Post Office to the harbor of the same name. This harbor lies between the southern part of Bartlett's Island and Mount Desert, and the place is of no special consequence only as being one of the numerous Post Offices on the Island, and the little village of which it is the centre. It is called Pretty Marsh in the early plantation records.

BASS HARBOR.

From Pretty Marsh Harbor, the road soon passes into the town of Tremont, on the westerly side of Seal Cove Pond, and not following the trend of the shore, passes Sawyer's Cove, Seal Cove and Post Office, and several other minor coves and points, to West Tremont Post Office, thence around by way of Duck Cove to Tremont Post Office, situated near the head of Bass Harbor. This harbor is formed by a long cove of irregular shape penetrating Mount Desert Island at its southwestern extremity. The upper portion of the cove is bare at low water. From Tremont Post Office a road runs southerly on the east side of the harbor to Bass Harbor Head where is a light-house, and terminates there. It is thickly settled upon this road, and to visit the light-house, which is a brick tower twenty-six feet high, would make about five miles extra travel down and back.

SOUTHWEST HARBOR.

From Tremont Post Office, across to the head of Southwest Harbor is about two miles. Here is a post office, several fine hotels— the Freeman, Island, Ocean, Claremont, Stanley, Dirigo and Sea Wall Houses—and here the night should be spent. Southwest Harbor is one of the best havens on the coast, and has been a place of note for many years. It was near here that the Jesuit mission was established years before the Pilgrims landed at Plymouth. It was here also that a few years ago, the Russian man-of-war, the "Cimbria," lay, which excited so much interest and curiosity throughout the state and country. Southwest Harbor lies just to the southward of the entrance to Somes' Sound, and is protected from northerly and northeasterly winds by Greening's Island. There are several passages leading into this harbor, one on the northern and one on the southern side of Bunker's Ledge, one between Little Cranberry and Sutton's Islands, and one between Great Cranberry and Mount Desert Islands.

SOMESVILLE.

Passing northerly by the head of Norwood's Cove, Flying and Dog Mountains are left on the right and Beach Mountain on the left, when the route is along by the eastern shore of Echo Lake, a beautiful sheet of water something over two miles long, Somesville is soon reached, a pleasant village with neat houses and a few cottages of summer residents. There is a good landing here at high water. Passing round at the head of Somes' Sound, the route by way of Northeast Harbor and Seal Harbor has already been described. The distance to be travelled by this route is not far from sixty miles. About two miles from Somesville

MOUNT DESERT, LOOKING UP SOMES'S SOUND

on the road to the narrows is " Town Hill " a thriving little village with stores, churches and a post office. A line of telegraph poles is on one side of this road, and of telephone poles on the other, both extending from Bar Harbor to Ellsworth. Excursions to Southwest Harbor can, if preferred, be more direct from Bar Harbor by buck-board or other vehicle, or the team and party may be taken to Southwest Harbor on one of the steamers plying between these points and then be driven back by way of Echo Lake and Somesville. Still another pleasant way is to charter one of the numerous small steamers plying in the bay, and the trip may be made more interesting by taking music and a lunch along.

THE "DESERT MOUNTAINS."

The mountains of Mount Desert Island are deserving of something more than a passing notice. In the scenery along the Atlantic coast, they are unique, and as great natural objects they are indeed wonderful. They cover more than a third part of the entire area of the Island, and have thirteen distinct peaks. They have the peculiarities of the mountains in other portions of the State, of being precipitous at the south and east, and sloping towards the north and west. They also exhibit diluvial markings and other evidence of glacial action. Green Mountain has already been spoken of; it is the largest, broadest and highest of the group, extending from Duck Brook to Otter Creek, a distance of nearly six miles. On the northeast is a bold spur which, though of the same mountain, takes the name of Dry Mountain. The ascent of this mountain affords vigorous and healthful exercise, the distance from Bar Harbor to the summit by way of Mount Kebo, being only about four miles.

NEWPORT MOUNTAIN.

This mountain is the most easterly of the group, and is situated between the Schooner Head and Otter Creek roads. On the summit is a small pond. Its cliffs towards the sea are steep and rugged, rising in grim rampart and solid bastian against the fury of terrific gales that sometimes come from this quarter. The foot of this mountain is only two and a half miles from Bar Harbor, and the ascent is gradual and easy. The top is a long flat ridge, and its nearness to the sea renders the view especially attractive.

MOUNT KEBO.

This little mountain is situated between Bar Harbor and Green Mountain, and its ascent is a favorite walk. To the summit is but little more than two miles from Bar Harbor, and many who would hesitate about climbing the higher elevations, are easily persuaded to undertake this. The site of an old mill at the base is a pleasant and romantic spot, while the view from the top is picturesque rather than grand, it being somewhat limited on account of the higher peaks by which it is partially surrounded.

" BEEHIVE."

This mountain is situated south of Newport and between it and the Peak of Otter. It is near to Great Head and is over five hundred feet above the sea. The " Bowl," a small pond on its northern slope, is four hundred and ten feet high. The Peak of Otter which is at the south and near to the Beehive is of about the same height.

PEMETIC MOUNTAIN.

This mountain, whose name perpetuates the Indian name of the Island, is situated southwest of Green Mountain, Turtle Lake whose waters flow into Eagle Lake, lying between. The best way to reach it is by boat up Eagle Lake to the beach at the head. The ascent from here is quite laborious and occupies a couple of hours. This mountain affords a finer view of the islands situated at the south and southwest, than does Green Mountain itself.

SARGENT'S MOUNTAIN.

This is a long mountain situated more nearly than any other at the center of Mount Desert Island. The foot of this mountain may be reached either by boat or carriage from Bar Harbor. By the latter method, the route is route is by the Somesville and Northeast Harbor roads. The task of reaching the summit is not an easy one, and none but the vigorous should undertake it. In the ascent, ledge rises above ledge, with thickets and tracts of fallen timber intervening, but when the summit is reached, the reward is ample. The top occupies a large area full of rifts and deep chasms, showing great disturbance of the rocky formation. The Lake of the Clouds is a little body of water an acre or so in area, and said to be very deep. It is situated in what seems to be an ancient crater, though there are no signs of volcanic rocks. Geologists have noted the resemblance of this to the Swiss mountains which have been shaped by glacial action. At some remote period, this entire Island and opposite mainland must have been the theater of active glacial action. The views from many parts of this mountain are very fine. An easier ascent and descent is said to be by way of Jordan's Pond.

OTHER MOUNTAINS.

The mountains already mentioned are the principal ones in the easterly part of the Island. Between Mount Kebo and Eagle Lake are Great Hill and White Cap, and north of Eagle Lake are the Interlaken

Hill and McFarland's and Young's Mountains, but none of them are as important as those already mentioned. South of Jordan's Pond are the "Triads" and the Cleft. On the easterly side of Somes' Sound is Brown's Mountain nearly nine hundred feet high, and quite precipitous in several places, and on the westerly side and bordering on the Sound are Robinson's, Dog and Flying Mountains. Beach Mountain is west of Dog Mountain, and Carter's Nubbles are north of the former. On the westerly side of the Island, between Great and Seal Cove Ponds, in the town of Tremont, are the Western Mountains, which overlook Penobscot Bay. The west peak is 1,073 feet high and the eastern 971. Like other mountains in this region, they present ragged and precipitous faces in certain directions, and are prominent objects from the sea. Their summits shut out the views of the western part of the Island and Penobscot Bay, from the top of Green Mountain. The summits of all these mountains as well as their northern slopes, were once covered by a dense growth of wood, but fire and storm have destroyed most of them. Fire and flood have also destroyed and carried away a large part of the shallow soil which supported the forest growths, leaving the sides and summits for the most part bare of vegetation. But to the inward bound mariner, the aspect of these mountains has ever been a solid wall of granite, precipitous and frowning, perpendicular or beetle-browed, and it is no wonder that when Champlain in his *pattache*, coasted along here nearly three centuries ago, and saw these bold peaks rising as it were out of the bosom of the ocean, should name the place the " Isle of the Desert Mountains." And thus they will ever remain; and while the Island may become dotted all over with summer cottages, while the rough and waste places may be changed to gardens and beautiful lawns, while all around and beneath them may be made to bud and blossom as the rose, these everlasting mountains will remain as they are, wild and weird yet majestic and grand, enduring monuments of the stupendous forces of nature.

CANTILEVER BRIDGE, OVER ST. JOHN RIVER AT ST. JOHN, N. B.

Opened for traffic October 1, 1885. The first through cantilever bridge ever built. Trains of the All-Rail Line cross this bridge and arrive at and depart from the new station of the Intercolonial Railway at St. John.

Mount Desert History.

SUCH a wonderful combination of scenery as that found upon the Island of Mount Desert, must have made a deep impression upon the minds of the early navigators as they pursued their way westwardly through the Gulf of Maine. In many respects it is unexcelled by any combination of natural views on the entire North Atlantic coast. Here upon one hundred square miles of territory are found thirteen mountain peaks varying in height from 700 to 1,500 feet above the sea level, seventeen ponds or lakes from a few acres to several square miles in area, deep gorges, and picturesque glens, bold promontories and broad stretches of forest, sparkling streams of water, with bays, harbors, coves and indentations of every variety and form. Besides all these natural objects, there are situated in various parts of the Island, sunny slopes, plateaus more or less broad, rocky ridges and headlands, affording sites for cottages to suit every taste and fancy. Mount Desert is the largest island on the New England coast. Its mountains can be seen sixty miles at sea, and are remarkable as being the first land mark of seamen. The Indians called the Island "Pemetic," a word which signifies "at the head " and which is perpetuated in the name of one of the Island Mountains. It was a favorite resort of the savages, where in the forests, they hunted for fur and food animals, and in the inlets and coves they took fin and shellfish in great quantities.

The discovery of Mount Desert Island, its early settlement as well as its subsequent history, are subjects of absorbing interest. It constituted a part of the ancient Acadia, for the possession of which there was a contest more or less sanguinary between England and France which lasted for more than a hundred and thirty years. The French founded their claim on the discovery of this coast by Verazzano in 1524, on the discovery and occupancy of Canada by Cartier, in 1535, and on the grant to De Monts in 1603. The English claim was based upon the discovery of Cabot in 1497, upon the occupancy of Newfoundland by Gilbert in 1553, by the subsequent voyage and landings of Gosnold, Pring, and Waymouth and others, by the charter to the Popham colony in 1606, and the occupancy of the soil by that colony in 1607. An account of this contest belongs to the domain of general history, and may be found in various historical works. It must answer for our present purpose to give an account of the early grant, and a brief outline of its subsequent history. There is no doubt that the several navigators who sailed along our coast prior to 1604, were struck with the unique appearance of this Island with its numerous mountain peaks, but their account of the entire coast is very meagre, and but little was written of any given point.

It was on the 8th day of November in the year of Grace 1603, that Henry, King of France, granted to his " well-beloved Sieur de Monts, in ordinary of his Bed Chamber, the territory known as Acadia, described as extending from the 40th to the 46th degree of north latitude and within this extent, or any part thereof, as far inland as might be practicable, to establish, extend and make known the king's name, power and authority and thereunto, subject, cause to submit and obey all the people of the said land, etc." This patent having no other boundaries than the degrees of latitude mentioned, embraced the American coast from the Island of Cape Breton to the Hudson river. The following winter De Monts equipped two vessels and accompanied by Samuel Champlain who had explored the St. Lawrence river the preceding year, sailed for his new possessions, March 7, 1604. After various explorations and the discovery of the river which De Monts named St. John, the name it still bears, he came to the waters of Passamaquoddy Bay and ascended the Schoodic River to a small island named by him the "St.Croix," and which he selected for a resting place. It was while stopping at this island that De Monts sent Champlain on an exploring expedition along the coast. Starting the second day of September, 1604, with a *pattache* of seventeen or eighteen tons, twelve sailors, and two savages as guides, Champlain sailed along the coast. " passing by a great quantity of islands, shallows and reefs which extend seaward in places more than four leagues;" again quoting his own language: " This same day we passed quite near an island which is some four or five leagues long, and were nearly lost on a little rock just under water which made a small hole in our bark near the keel. The island is very high and so cleft in places that at sea it appears as if seven or eight mountains were ranged side by side. I have named this island, *L'isle des Monts-deserts* (the isle of the desert mountains), its latitude is 44½°." The place selected by De Monts for his colony was at Port Royal, so named by Champlain, and was opposite Goat Island on the north bank of the river of Port Royal, and six miles distant from the present town of Annapolis, N. S. Without accomplishing much, De Monts returned to France and we hear no more of him.

One of the leading objects had in view by the French in the colonization of Acadia was the conversion of the Indians to the Catholic faith.

To that end the colonists were generally accompanied by priests, some of whom were those known as of the Order of Jesus, or Jesuits. De Monts was succeeded in Acadia by his associate in his voyage, Jean de Biencourt, a French baron, who having occasion to revisit France left the affairs of the colony in charge of his son. Meanwhile a French lady of wealth and influence, had formed the design of establishing in Acadia a spiritual despotism of which the Jesuits were to be the rulers and she the patroness. Henry of France had been assassinated and the queen mother ruled in his stead during the minority of her son. She favored the views of Madame de Guerchville, and rendered material aid. A vessel was fitted out at Honfleur and the command given to M. de la Saussaye who was to be governor of the colony. Among those who embarked in this vessel were two Jesuits named Quantin and Du Thet. They had orders to go to Port Royal and being re-enforced by Fathers Biard and Masse, to proceed to Pentagoet (the Penobscot) and there to found their colony. Arriving at Port Royal, they took on board the two Jesuits, their servant and luggage, and proceeded westward along the coast. Father Biard had visited Pentagoet the year previous, and now acted as guide. When off Grand Menan, a thick fog closed in upon them which lasted for two days, and when it lifted they put into a harbor on the "easterly side of Mount Desert" Island.*

This harbor was secure and commodious with deep water, and was regarded as a favorable place for a colony. To this place they gave the name of St. Sauveur (St. Saviour). There are many reasons for supposing that the place selected by the colonists was Fernald's Point, near the entrance to Somes' Sound. It is a delightful spot sheltered by Flying Mountain from the base of which it slopes gently to the water. It has been occupied by the Fernalds as a farm for three generations and the house is one of the oldest in the vicinity. The springs of water spoken of by Biard in his recently published journal, where the Jesuit colony slaked their thirst and with which they performed their ablutions and cooked their food, are still flowing upon Fernald's Point. The harbor for depth of water, capacity and safety fully answers the description given of it by the Jesuits.

Historians differ as to the time when this island was settled.

---

* Biard in his journal distinctly states that the landing was made upon the easterly side, but there is no spot on that side which answers to his description of the place, while Fernald's Point is exactly described by him. He says: "This place is a beautiful hill, sloping gently from the seashore and supplied with water by a spring on each side. It fronts the south and east towards Pentagoet Bay. The port and harbor are the finest possible, in a position commanding the entire coast; the harbor especially is smooth as a pond, being shut in by the large Island of Mount Desert; besides being surrounded by certain small islands which break the force of the winds and waves, and fortify the entrance. It is large enough to hold any fleet and is navigable for the largest ships up to a cable's length from the shore."

Williamson gives the date as 1609, and says "it is supposed the place selected by Biard ad Massse, was on the western side of the Pool—a part of the sound which stretches from the southeasterly side to the heart of the island." He adds: "Here they constructed and fortified an habitation, planted a garden and dwelt five years, entering with great zeal and untiring perserverance upon the work of converting the natives to Christianity." On the other hand, Hannay in his History of Acadia, says the vessel which conveyed the colony, including Biard and Masse, to St. Sauveur, sailed from France on the 12th of March, 1613, and reached Cape La Have May 16th. This would fix their arrival at Mount Desert sometime in June of 1613, and would give them a residence there of brief duration*. Hannay says of the colony: "All the company were speedily engaged in clearing ground and erecting buildings. La Saussaye was advised by the principal colonists to erect sufficient fortification before commencing to cultivate the soil, but he disregarded the advice, and nothing was completed in the way of defense, except the raising of a small palisaded structure when a storm burst upon the colony which was little expected by its founders." All accounts agree as to the time and manner in which the colony was broken up.

Among the persons who were in the habit of visiting these shores at that period was Samuel Argal. Concerning the character of this man, various opinions have been expressed, but that he was a skillful navigator there can be no doubt. It was he who discovered a more direct passage to Virginia and left the track of more ancient navigators. He was an adventurer of the Drake School, who never hesitated to plunder and rob those not of his own country. Argal became attached to the colony on the James River in Virginia in 1609, and frequently came to the coast of Maine in the interests of the colony for the purpose of taking fish. In 1613 while in the vicinity of Penobscot Bay, he learned from the Indians of the French proceedings at St. Sauveur, and resolved to break up the colony. It made no difference to Argal that England and France were then at peace. The Jamestown colony, which he represented, regarded all encroachments upon their territory as acts of hostility and assumed the right to keep off all intruders. Argals's approach greatly surprised the French, but having a ship and a barque in the harbor, and a light entrenchment on shore, they did what they could to defend themselves. Argal attacked the place with musketry, and at the second discharge, Du Thet fell mortally wounded, and two young men named Lemoine and Neveau were drowned. The French were easily overpowered and fifteen of the colonists, including Fathers Biard and Quantin, were taken to Vir-

---

* Biard's Journal shows that both he and Masse were at Port Royal when the vessel bringing Saussaye and the other colonists arrived from France, and does not mention any previous residence on Mount Desert Island.

ginia where they were to have the free exercise of their religion with permission to return to France at the end of a year; the remaining fifteen, including La Saussaye and Father Masse, were put in a shallop and directed to go in search of some French vessel which would take them home. On the coast of Nova Scotia they found a vessel which took them to St. Malo. On arriving at Jamestown, the Virginia colonists approved the doings of Argal, and resolved to send him to destroy all the French settlements in Acadia. He having fitted out a small fleet, first visited St. Sauveur where he destroyed the cross erected by the Jesuits and set up another in its place with the name of the King of England inscribed upon it. He also destroyed all the buildings the French had erected and changed the beautiful spot to a desolate waste. Proceeding to St. Croix he destroyed the buildings left there, and then proceeded to invest Port Royal. The people were at work in the fields, and the first knowledge they had that enemies were near, was the smoke of their burning homes. The destruction of the place was complete. Most of the French returned to France, but Biencourt refused to go, and spent the remainder of his days in the country, sometimes dwelling with the savages and at others in company with Charles de La Tour near Port Royal, but little is known of his subsequent life. This ends the story of the Jesuit occupancy of Mount Desert Island, and whether they were here five years, or only a part of a single year, it matters little now. The ashes of Du Thet repose at Fernald's Point which is the ancient St. Sauveur, and probably other relics of the French mission may be buried beneath the soil, but the description of the harbor, the admirable site for such a settlement, and the boiling springs in the vicinity are the only existing evidence by which we are able to locate the spot. More than two hundred and seventy years have passed since this little band of Christian workers was driven from St. Sauveur, but there is still a glamour about the spot, and an interest attaches to it which is possessed by no other place on the Maine coast. There were never any more devoted, self sacrificing, persistent workers in the missionary field, than the French Jesuits who came to the wilds of America to convert the savages to the Christian faith.

RESETTLEMENT.

The history of Mount Desert Island from the breaking up of the Jesuit Colony at St. Sauveur to the end of French domination in Acadia, possesses but few incidents of general interest. The contest for empire continued to be carried on between France and England, and there was no security for settlers upon the disputed territories, of either nationality. In April, 1688, for some consideration not now apparent, the King of France granted to M. la Motte Cadillac, the whole of Mount Desert with adjacent islands and lands bordering on Trenton River. This grant, though made void by subsequent events, was revived nearly a hundred years later. In 1762, in consideration of his "extraordinary services" the general Court of Massachusetts granted Mount Desert Island to Governor Bernard. Governor Bernard was a loyalist and when he left the country his property, including the territory of Mount Desert, was confiscated; but to his son a resident of Bath, who was a staunch whig throughout the war, half of his father's estate was restored. Meantime the claim of Cadillac was revived in the person of Mons. Bartholomew Gregoire, and his wife Maria Theresa who was the great-granddaughter of the original grantee. It was an old and doubtless obsolete claim, but at and immediately after the close of the Revolutionary war, the Government of Massachusetts was especially well disposed toward France and her citizens, and so, in 1787, the Great and General Court first naturalized the petitioners, and then gave them a quit-claim deed of the interest held by Massachusetts in the Island, it being one-half of it, reserving to actual settlers, lots of one hundred acres each. The petitioners settled here, and Theresa Gregoire died at Hull's Cove, on the spot now occupied by the large brick mansion house, in 1810. Many of the settlers on the Island hold title deeds based upon this grant.

The contest between England and France for the possession of Acadia, prevented the settlement of any part of it by the English until the fall of Quebec in 1759, put an end to French domination over all the disputed territory, and to the bloody Indian wars which had been waged with more or less severity for more than one hundred and thirty years.

It is generally conceded that Abraham Somes, Jr., was the first permanent settler on this Island, though James Richardson came either at the same time, or very soon after. There may have been straggling settlements previous to that by Somes and Richardson of those engaged in fishing and hunting, but if so they were only temporary residents, whose names have not come down to us. Somes*, who gave his name to the Sound and to the village at its head, was of Gloucester, Mass. He was in the habit of visiting this region, prior to his removal here, in a Chebacco boat (so-called from Chebacco, a town in Massachusetts, now called Essex, where such boats were built), for the purpose of rifting pine into staves which he took back to Gloucester and manufactured into barrels, etc. In 1762, he took his family along with him, and for the first winter they lived in the boat, near the head of the Sound. The next season he built a house on the shore and moved into it, being the first

---

* He was the son of Abraham and Martha Emerson Somes who were married at Gloucester in 1730, and was the fourth in descent from Morris Somes who was born in 1614, and with his wife Margerie was among the early settlers at Gloucester, on Cape Ann. Morris Somes was the common ancestor of all the New England families of this name.

settler. His numerous progeny are among the most respectable people of the Island.

The patriarch lived to be over eighty years of age and when the died he was buried at Somesville. His wife was Hannah, daughter of Samuel Herrick of Gloucester.

The records of Mount Desert as a municipality begin in 1776 and the first meeting called was for the purpose of choosing a committee of Correspondence, Inspection and Safety. This meeting was held on the 30th day of March, 1776, at the house of Stephen Richardson; Josiah Black was chosen moderator and James Richardson* clerk. The committee of Correspondence, Inspection and Safety consisted of Ezra Young, Levi Higgins, Stephen Richardson, Isaac Bunker and Thomas Richardson.

Mount Desert was incorporated as the sixty-eighth town in the State, Feb., 1789, and included Barlett's, Robinson's, Beach and the Cranberry Islands. At that time, the several places numbered about seven hundred inhabitants. The inhabitants were loyal to the patriot cause during the struggle for independence, almost to a man, and suffered much both from the enemy and for the necessaries of life. The first English child born in the town is said to have been George, son of James Richardson in August, 1763, and the first recorded marriage took place August 4, 1774.

The first representative to the General Court was David Wasgalt in 1805. In 1796 the town was divided and the northern part took the name of Eden. The Cranberry Isles were incorporated as a town in 1830, and in 1848 the southerly part of Mount Desert was incorporated by the name of " Mansell,"† and the name changed to Tremont the same year.

PHYSICAL FEATURES.

Mount Desert Island is very irregular in outline, its shores being everywhere indented with bays, coves, creeks and inlets. Its extreme length from north to south, from Hadley's Point in Eden to Bass Harbor Head Light House in Tremont, is about fifteen and one-half miles, and its greatest width from east to west, from Great Head to a point east of Thrumbcap Island, is thirteen miles. Its average length is about twelve miles, and its width nine miles. It is separated from the main land on the north and northeast by French-

---

* James Richardson, of Gloucester, settled at Mount Desert in 1763 and was the second settler at Somesville.

† Mount Desert was sometimes called " Mount Mansell " in honor of Sir Richard Mansell, a famous navigator. It was the first land in New England seen by Winthrop's fleet of immigrants in 1630 and is mentioned in Winthrop's Journal as "Mount Mansell."

man's Bay, and on the northwest and west, by Union River Bay and Bluehill Bay. Its nearest approach to the mainland is at the Narrows where a bridge seven hundred feet in length connects it with the town of Trenton. But for the numerous small islands which intervene, there would be an open sea view toward the southeast and south; at many points along the shore, the view is unobstructed in these directions, and nothing meets the eye but a wide waste of waters. It has thirteen distinct mountain peaks and several other bluffs of lesser height. These mountains are situated in the central part of the Island from east to west, the chain being divided by Somes' Sound and the larger number of peaks being east of this Sound, and between it and the Bar Harbor side. The heights of the elevations on Mount Desert Island, above mean high water, are given in the following table, and are mostly compiled from the coast survey reports.

		FEET.			FEET.
Green Mountain,	- -	1527	Robinson's Mountain,	-	700
Sargent's "	- - -	1344	Dog "	- -	670
Dry "	- -	1268	The Beehive, - - -		540
Pemetic "	- - -	1262	Great Pond Hill, - - -		540
Newport "	- -	1060	The Cleft { North,	- -	610
			{ South,	- -	460
Western " { W. Peak,		1073	Peak of Otter, - - -		506
{ E. Peak,		971			
White Cap, - - - -		925	Carter's Nubble,	- -	480
Brown's Mountain, - -		860	Interlaken Hill, - - -		462
Bubbles { North,	- -	845	Mt. Kebo, - - - -		405
{ South,	- -	730			
Beach Mt., - - - -		855	Jordan's Hills { North,	-	340
			{ South,	-	360
McFarland's Mountain, -		761	Flying Mountain, - - -		300
Great Hill, - - - -		748	Bald Mountain, - -		250
The Triads { East, - -		720			
{ North, -		688	High Head Mountain,	-	208
{ South, - -		600			
			Burnt Mt., - - - -		175
Young's, - - - -		706	Mt. Gibbon, - - -		160
			Otter Cliff, - - - -		112

These numerous peaks constitute a vast watershed, and as a consequence there are numerous ponds or lakes situated in various parts of the island. The best known of these is Eagle Lake so named by Church, the artist, situated about three miles west of Bar Harbor. Its principal watersheds are the Green, Dry, Sargent's and Pemetic Mountains, with the Bubbles and White Cap. Its outlet is called Duck Brook, and it supplies the water for the village of Bar Harbor. This lake is 2½ miles long and ¾ of a mile wide. It is navigable for steamers and is part of the thoroughfare between Bar Harbor and the Green Mountain Railway. Jordan's Pond is south of Eagle Lake, and separated from it by the Bubbles. Its waters flow into Long Pond which is situated on the southerly side of Mount Desert, near Seal Harbor. The largest pond on the Island situated partly in the westerly part of the town of Mount Desert and north part of Tremont, is Great Pond which is over four miles long, and has numerous little bays and coves. Echo Lake is situated about equal distance from Great Pond and Somes' Sound, and is two miles long by half a mile wide. It is on the road between Somesville and Southwest Harbor. Hadlock Pond is a small sheet of water on the road between Somesville and Northeast Harbor. Turtle Lake is situated between Green and Pemetic Mountains, and its waters flow into Eagle Lake. Seal Cove Pond is toward the western part of the Island, and flows into Seal Cove. Besides these, there are the Lake Wood, Pond of Witch Hollow, Somes' Pond, The "Bowl" and several others. The summer level of some of these lakes and ponds is as follows:

	FEET.		FEET.
The Bowl, - - -	410	Echo Lake, - - - -	90
Turtle Lake, - - -	375	Long Pond, - - -	58
Eagle Lake, - - -	275	Seal Cove Pond, - - -	30
Jordan's Pond,- - -	195		

Some of these island mountains are joined at their base, while others are so near each other as to leave only a narrow gorge between. The road from Bar Harbor to Otter Creek is between Dry and Newport Mountains whose bases approach each other so nearly as to leave little more than space for a wagon road. Nearly all the roads on the Island running from north to south, have mountains either on one or both sides for much of the way.

Somes' Sound is a remarkable feature in the make up of Mount Desert Island. Beginning near Southwest Harbor, it penetrates northwardly into the land for nearly seven miles, almost bisecting the Island. Its average width is less than a mile, and for much of the way it is overshadowed by mountains. On the westerly side are Flying, Dog and Robinson's Mountains, and on the east Brown's extended summit nearly nine hundred feet high. In sailing up this sound one who did not know to the contrary, could easily persuade himself that he had entered a large river. Many of its features, especially its deep dark waters, and the overhanging and echoing cliffs, recall the Saguenay river of Canada with its grand, almost awful scenery.

A striking feature of Mount Desert Island is its rock-bound shore which extends nearly around it, rising at some points into bluffs with perpendicular or everhanging walls, against which the waves of ocean dash with ceaseless fury. The material of which these rocky bluffs are composed, acted upon by the waves and salt water, falls down in broken fragments which are rolled and pounded, and in some places when the tide is out, the shore under the bluffs is covered with them in every fantastic form. The sea-wall at Southwest Harbor which, after an off the coast storm, is frequently fifteen feet high, is one of the most interesting of such embankments found along the coast. At Northeast Harbor, the travelled road is for some distance, over a sea-wall composed of rounded stones from the size of a goose egg and upward to three or four pounds in weight.

GEOLOGICAL.

The geology of Mount Desert Island is very interesting. As in other portions of the State, the southern brows of the lofty granitic hills, are everywhere crushed and broken into fearful precipices, while their sides turned to the north present plains of greater breadth, and dip at vastly less angles down towards the level country beyond. The great boulders lie at their southern feet, and those specifically the same, but of less magnitude, are transported the farthest off, and are more worn and rounded. It seems to have been the special business of the great denuding agent, to cover the barren surface with soils, which soils are the results of local detritus—gravels, clays and sands, crushed and ground out of the detached rocks. In speaking of the geology of this region, Prof. Hitchcock says:

"Another large basin of mica schist is in the southern part of Hancock county, three sides certainly, resting upon granite. This granite is shaped like a great horse-shoe, one end being at Mount Desert Island, running through Sullivan, Franklin, Number Eight, North Ellsworth, Orland, Surry, Bluehill and Sedgwick, to its other end on Deer Isle; and within this curve the mica schist is situated. The character of the rock is gneissoid, and sometimes talcose and again like siliceous slate. The country within this area is low and rolling, while the great granite curve is composed of high mountains. After this depression had been formed by the upheaval of the granitic ranges around the lowlands, the schists were deposited in it, though in this case the schist deposit failed to reach anywhere near to the top of the ridge or basin. The rocks in this great valley belong to one formation, and were formed during the same geological period."

Prof. Hitchcock found that Mount Desert Island is composed chiefly of granitic, unstratified rocks, though an occasional mass of an obscure siliceous slate appears. An interesting quartz vein is found along the shore at Bar Harbor, opposite Bar Island, extending for a mile and a half. Going back from the shore, it is much acted upon by the weather and would hardly be recognized as the same rock. There is a dike of trap at Hull's

Cove containing limestone. Green Mountain is a mass of red granite, or at least, it appears so at the summit and on its sides. It is of the variety known as protogine in which a talcose mineral takes the place of mica in the ordinary granite, and it is probable that nearly all the so-called granite of the Island is protogine. The dip of large plates of this rock on the top of Green Mountain is 60 N.W., while near Eagle Lake, they are nearly perpendicular. Occasionally a dike of trap is found on this mountain, and what is true of the structure of Green Mountain is probably true of others. Near Otter Creek at the base of the "Bee-hive," a quarry of red granite is being successfully worked. Paving stones for New York City are being quarried in great quantity on the westerly side of Somes' Sound; from the deck of the steamer, these quarries appeared to be of ordinary granite. Syenite, a form of granite in which hornblende is substituted for mica, is found in some places and a company lost a large sum in attempting to open a quarry of it.

Green Mountain which was once a United States Coast Survey Station is 1527 feet above the surrounding ocean, the highest point on the At-lantic Coast, between Lubec and the Rio Grande, and is the first land sighted by mariners when approaching this coast. From the summit the scene is grand—almost overwhelming. Here one gets a birds' eye view of more than three-fourths of the entire Island, including its harbors, bays, coves, sounds, lakes, ponds, mountains, forest, farms and villages; also of several towns on the mainland, numerous islands along the coast line, and a broad expanse of ocean. The Schoodic Mountains, Bluehill and the Camden Hills are seen in the distance, while in the opposite direction white sails gleaming in the sunlight glide smoothly over the azure sea. Language is inadequate to express the beauty and variety of the scenes here opened to view, and the emotions they awaken cannot be told in words; the impressions they make upon the mind are indelible, and remain as an unfading memorial of a most delightful and enjoyable occasion. The two grandest objects in nature, high mountains and a boundless ocean, here occupy the same horizon, and no earthly view can be more absorbing.

AGRICULTURAL RESOURCES.

The agriculture of Mount Desert Island is necessarily poor. The soil, as a rule, is thin and lacking in the elements of fertility. Formed of the detritus of the rocks composing the skeleton of the Island, its con-stituent elements are few and mostly of a siliceous kind. There is not much level surface and what there is is either sandy, or marshy and wet. Nature never intended this as an agricultural region. The climate also, is unsuited to high farming. Not so much on account of its high latitude as its nearness to the Atlantic and Arctic currents which strike the coast at this point. The water of the ocean here is nearly thirty degree colder than it is west of the mouth of the Kennebec. The change from winter to summer and from summer to winter is very gradual, and the period of uncertain weather is long, much longer than at other points in the same latitude away from the coast where farming is made a success. This period of irregular alternating of summer and winter days is the ruin of agricultural prosperity.* "Agriculture has always received some attention here, but the employment of the early settlers was chiefly lumbering and fishing. The ice business, granite quarrying, and catering to the wants of summer residents are the chief employments of the inhabitants of this island to-day, and will be in the future."

THE REAL NAME.

It would hardly seem necessary after quoting Champlain's statement with regard to the name of this Island and his reasons for so naming it, to call attention to the proper accentuation of the word "Desert," but there are still many who place the accent on the last syllable, a practice which has a tendency to obscure its meaning. We have seen that Champlain called the place, the "Isle of the Desert Mountains," and from this doubtless, it came to be called Mount Desert. The French words for this name are *Mont Desert*, the last word pronounced as though written *"dezer."* Now since we have substituted Mount for the French "Mont," why should we not give the word *Desert* which is written alike in French and English, the English accent? It is true Champlain did not call the Island a desert, only its mountains, but the words "Mount Desert" or "Desert Mount," convey the meaning intended by him, and the word Desert with the accent on the first syllable used in its ordinary sense of solitary, untilled, uninhabited, is part of the name. The fact that many of the natives of the Island accent the word differently and give a different significance to the terms employed by Champlain, proves nothing. We have Champlain's own statement that the name was intended to describe an island filled with solitary, uninhabited mountain wastes, and no words better described such a place than those used by him.

AS A SUMMER RESORT.

That Mount Desert Island with Bar Harbor as a rallying point and business center, is to become an immense summer resort, no one who has become acquainted with its peculiar adaption to that purpose, can for a moment doubt.

For fifty years it has been a summer resort in a certain degree, but its temporary residents had, up to twenty years ago, dwelt for the most part at Southwest Harbor. Somes' Sound, then as now, possessed pe-

* Survey of Hancock County, 1878.

culiar attractions for water excursions, the scenery along its indented shores being grand and beautiful. The harbor here was excellent and easily accessible, and this was the part of the Island first settled. Among the temporary residents at Southwest Harbor, were several artists who made this their favorite sketching ground. Later on, when the part of the Island had been transferred to canvas, F. E. Church and others found their way around the head of Somes' Sound to Eagle Lake, which Church thus named, to Bar Harbor. Finding the scenery here especially attractive, they engaged board and rooms with the farmers, and remained here through the season. This bold scenery transferred to canvas by Church, Brown, Morton, Hart and others, soon made the locality familiar to the residents of the large cities, and summer travel soon began to gravitate toward the eastern part of the Island. This was the beginning of Bar Harbor as a sea-side resort, and was less than twenty years ago. Now the palatial hotels, the millions of dollars invested in cottages, the almost fabulous prices at which real estate is sold in and around Bar Harbor, and the distinguished names such as Jay Gould, Wm. H. Vanderbilt, George B. McClellan, James G. Blaine and scores of others registered here during the past summer, indicate that this is to be *par excellence*, the fashionable quarter of the Island.

But other points have their peculiar attractions, and while Southwest Harbor more than holds its own, Northeast Harbor, Seal Cove, Somesville and many other places have their summer hotels, their cottages and more or less temporary residents. The Island is being surrounded by a cordon of invaders, and the time will come when all the land bordering on or near the sea, will be cut up into houselots for their use.

As before stated the extension of the Maine Central R.R. to Mount Desert has given a new impetus to travel to this great resort. From the 27th day of July, 1885, to the 10th day of October, 1885, the ferry-boat of that Company landed at Bar Harbor 6,939 people, and during the same time took away 8,304, the difference between those arriving and those leaving being accounted for by the arrival previous to time of keeping record. It will thus be seen that this Company handled over 15,000 passengers during the season, and the Portland, Bangor, Mount Desert and Machias Steamboat Company over 3,000 more. Already is Mount Desert Ferry a port of entry and during the year 1884 steamers were run to and from Digby and Annapolis, N. S., touching at Eastport and connecting with trains of the Maine Central and Windsor & Annapolis Railways, a service which is likely to be renewed any day and now large numbers of tourists travel between Bar Harbor and Campobello, via steamers to and from Machiasport thence by Lubec stages. At the height of the season the large numbers of little steamers plying between various points of the bay, and others engaged in excursion business together with the large steamers running to and from Bar Harbor, create quite a lively appearance, and then too, Bar Harbor is situated at just the right distance from New York, Boston or Portland to make a yachting cruise desirable, and hence may be seen here the most celebrated yachts of the country conveying hither their well-known owners and friends. At times also United States naval vessels are to be found here, making the social element of the place of the most delightful character. A grand yacht race is in contemplation as one of the attractions of Mount Desert another season. Enterprising parties at Bar Harbor have also had a steamer built to run during the summer months between Bar Harbor and Isle au Haut touching at Northeast and Southwest Harbors and other points en route, leaving Bar Harbor in the morning after the arrival of night train from Boston and returning to connect with night train from Bar Harbor to Boston, thus opening up another desirable locality as a resort and enabling visitors at Southwest and Northeast Harbors to connect with the trains without any trouble on their part ; a fact they will undoubtedly appreciate.

SORRENTO.

Another pleasant resort in prospect is Sorrento, Point Harbor, Maine, on one of the most attractive spots bordering the picturesque shores of Frenchman's Bay. It is situated on a peninsula extending from the main land of the northern shore of Frenchman's Bay, opposite to and within five minutes' sail of Mt. Desert Ferry, and twenty minutes' sail of Bar Harbor.

The scenery at Sorrento, and environments, is enchanting. The visitor is at once attracted and captivated by the grand beauty of the panoramic views of ocean and mountain, valley and forest, presenting themselves in all directions. From the eastern portion of the place is seen Flanders Bay, Bass Cove, the islands, farms and settlements in the village of East Sullivan and the Gouldsboro shore. Looking to the south is seen the Atlantic Ocean, its surface dotted with sail and steam vessels of various kinds and nationality, the numerous and charming islands, and Mount Desert looming up and expanding into magnificent proportions, and Bar Harbor with its palatial mansions and elegant cottages. To the westward may be seen Lamoine, Crabtree Neck—the proposed site for the Government Light-house—Hancock Point, Mount Desert Ferry, and the new and excellent hotel, the "Bluffs." To the north are seen the Sullivan Falls, West Sullivan, Sullivan Village and the St. John Hotel, from which place a most charming view of Frenchman's Bay may be obtained. While for a back ground, to complete the picture, are seen Schoodic Mountain, Trunk Mountains, Black Hills and the Catherine Mountains, the whole forming a charming combination and variety of scenery, rarely found in other sections of the country. Point Harbor, the landing place of Sorrento, is an ancient and historic harbor, and affords good shelter for vessels of all kinds, and is admitted to be one of the safest harbors on the coast of Maine. Sorrento is already attracting attention as a desirable place for summer residence, and bids fair to become a popular place of resort.

ISLAND HOUSE,

Southwest Harbor.   -   -   Mount Desert, Me.

This house is situated near the steamer landing, on the south side of the island, facing the ocean, with the whole range of mountains, thirteen in number, in form of a half-circle, in the rear; in front the cluster of beautiful islands that make the harbor, and afford a fine, spacious and safe bay for sailing or rowing. The facilities for brook, lake, or sea fishing are unexcelled on the island, and all the most desirable excursions and drives, both along the rugged shores and among the mountains are of easy access from this point. Green Mountain Railway is only two and one-half hours' ride from Southwest Harbor, over a fine road. The view from the cupola of this house is magnificent. This house has been enlarged, newly furnished and improved, and is now one of the best on the south side of the island. It is supplied with pure water and perfect sewerage. Terms moderate. Open about July 1st.

For terms, circulars, etc., apply to

H. H. CLARK, Proprietor.

P. O. Address,
S. W. Harbor, Hancock Co., Me.

GRAND CENTRAL HOTEL
BAR HARBOR ME.,
• MT. DESERT. •
R. HAMOR & SONS, Proprietors.

This house has a view of both mountains and ocean, and is within two minutes, walk of R. R. Depot. There are two hundred large and airy sleeping rooms; also, large parlors, music room, dining hall, and office provided with large brick fire-places, for wood fires. The house is supplied with pure water, and all sanitary improvements. First-class cooks; tables supplied with the best the market affords. We endeavor to make this one of the best hotels in Bar Harbor. **R. HAMOR & SONS, Bar Harbor, Me.**

ATLANTIC HOUSE, Bar Harbor, Maine.

This favorably located hotel, situated on a plot of four acres, commands superior views of Mountains, Islands and Bay, and is first-class in all its appointments. Entirely remodeled, it has Electric Bells, new Bath Rooms, and all modern improvements, including pure water and good drainage. It has a large and tastefully graded lawn with Tennis Court, for the accommodation of guests. Telegraph and Telephone connnection.

W. E. RICHARDSON, Manager.   . T. HAMOR, **Proprietor.**

West End Hotel.

This Hotel is one of the largest and best constructed hotels at Bar Harbor, and surpasses all in its location ; overlooking the Harbor, Frenchman's Bay, and a beautiful view of the Mountains, and of many of the finest cottages; and having connected with it three large Tennis Courts. It has one hundred and fifty rooms, with all modern improvements—Electric Lights, Gas, Passenger Elevator, Electric Bells, Steam Heat, Steam Laundry, Fire Escapes. The *cuisine* receives most particular attention, as also everything conducive to the comforts of the guests. No pains will be spared to make this hotel first-class in all respects.

O. M. SHAW & SON, Proprietors.

The Boston & Albany R.R.

IS THE ONLY LINE

Having Through Car Service from

St. Louis and Chicago to Boston,

Via N. Y. C. & H. R. R.R.

Only Line running **four** Express trains week days, and **two** Sundays, between

NEW YORK and BOSTON.

THE MALVERN

AND COTTAGES,

Bar Harbor, - Maine.

OTTO E. HANSEN, Manager

CLAREMONT & HOUSE,

SOUTHWEST HARBOR,

MOUNT DESERT, MAINE.

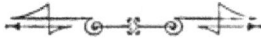

Located on Clark's Point, directly opposite Northeast Harbor, and commanding an uninter-
rupted view up Somes' Sound.

This beautiful sheet of water, pronounced by critics the most picturesque in America, is a deep indentation nearly bisecting Mt. Desert Island. On either side extend the rugged but water-worn and rounded mountains which have made Mt. Desert famous. Upon their sides the passing clouds cause ceaseless play of light and shade, or hide their summits in a wreath of mist.

Towards the East the view discloses Mt. Desert's Southern rock-bound shore, and the adjacent islands with the open sea beyond. From this situation all the more interesting features of Mt. Desert, such as Bar Harbor, the Sea Wall, Echo Lake, Schooner Head, the views from the various mountain tops, are of easy access by either boat or drive, while the confusion and crowding at Bar Harbor may be avoided.

This House was new last season, and is strictly first-class in all its appointments. From the high ground on which the house stands the land slopes gently to the water, where a sandy beach affords excellent bathing facilities.

Boats and yachts under the supervision of competent and trustworthy men, are furnished for fishing or sailing excursions.

An excellent stable connected with this house, furnishes means for driving through some of the most magnificent scenery in America.

At the rear of the house is a shady grove of evergreen trees. An abundant supply of water, pronounced by Prof. F. L. Bartlett of Portland, in his analysis, "one of the pure waters seldom found in any country," and possessing high medicinal properties is derived from a deep artesian well. By the use of this unfailing source every modern convenience is secured, all the sanitary arrangements being of the highest order, and furnished with the latest appliances. The systems of drainage and ventilation are perfect.

The large, airy rooms of this house are neatly and most comfortably furnished throughout. The table set is unexcelled by any on the island. This house is nearest to the landing (within five minutes' walk) where daily connection is made with Boston by steamer, or by rail via Mt. Desert Ferry.

Telegraph and Telephone a short distance from the hotel.

Our terms are reasonable. To secure rooms or learn terms, address,

J. H. PEASE, Proprietor.

The Rodick

Main Street, Bar Harbor.

D. RODICK & SONS, Proprietors.

Largest hotel in Maine. Four hundred sleeping rooms belonging to the hotel and cottages connected.

Complete drainage and water supply; highest elevation; beautiful and extensive views; largest lawn and grounds of any hotel at Bar Harbor; lighted with gas and has modern improvements.

Our Halls, Parlors, Office and Dining Hall afford ample accommodation for one thousand persons.

Prices according to size and location of rooms. Liberal terms by the season.

FALMOUTH HOTEL,

PORTLAND, MAINE.

J. K. MARTIN, Proprietor.

"The Falmouth" is one of the most elegant and perfect Hotels in the United States. Its location being near the public buildings, banks and principal stores, is the finest and most desirable in the city. Every improvement known to modern ingenuity and skill will be found at "The Falmouth," while its *CUISINE* and service is unexceptionable. The hotel is furnished in elegant and costly style; rooms single or *en suite;* private drawing-rooms and dining-rooms. Rates are graded at $2.00, $2.50, $3.00, $3.50, $4.00 and $4.50 per day, according to size and location of rooms.

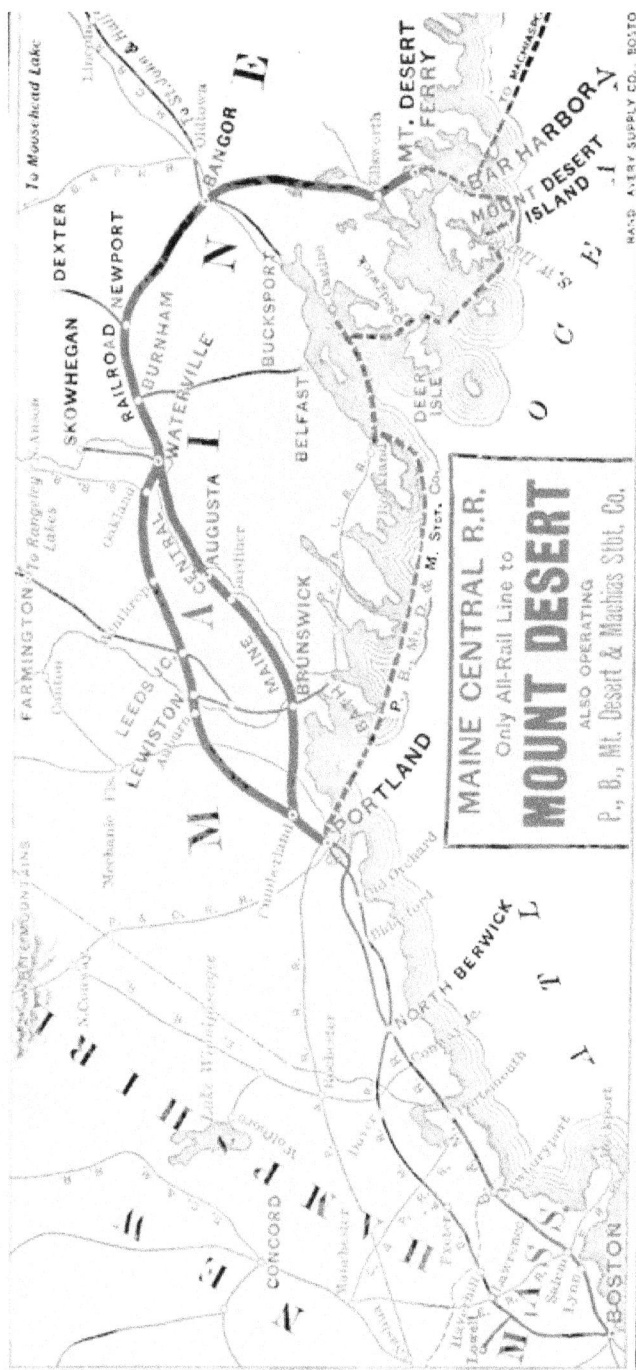

MAINE CENTRAL R.R.

Only All-Rail Line to

MOUNT DESERT

ALSO OPERATING

P., B., Mt. Desert & Machias Stbt. Co.